THE PLIERS

LEARNING ABOUT TOOLS

David and Patricia Armentrout

The Rourke Book Co., Inc.
Vero Beach, Florida 32964

PHOTO CREDITS
©East Coast Studios: cover, title, pages 8, 10, 13, 15;
© Armentrout: pages 4, 18; © Sears, Roebuck & Co.: page 7;
© Stanley Tools: page 12; © ORMC: page 17; © NASA: page 21

Library of Congress Cataloging-in-Publication Data

Armentrout, Patricia, 1960-
  The pliers / by Patricia Armentrout and David Armentrout.
     p. cm. — (Learning about tools)
  Includes index.
  ISBN 1-55916-120-5
    1. Pliers—Juvenile literature.   [1. Pliers. 2. Tools.]
I. Armentrout, David, 1962- . II. Title.   III. Series.
TJ1201. T65A76 1995
621.9' 8—dc20
                                                94–46473
                                                   CIP
                                                   AC

Printed in the USA

TABLE OF CONTENTS

Pliers	5
Slip Joint Pliers	6
Locking Pliers	9
Long Nose Pliers	11
Electrical Pliers	14
Pliers for Medical Use	16
Special Pliers	19
Caring for Tools	20
Safety	22
Glossary	23
Index	24

PLIERS

Pliers are tools that help us grip and hold onto objects. Some pliers even provide cutting power.

Basic pliers have two metal pieces held together by a **pivot** (PIV-et) pin.

The short end of the plier, which holds or grips objects, is called the jaw. The longer end is the handle. The handle is squeezed to bring the jaw or cutting edge together.

Pliers are often used by fishermen to remove a fish hook

SLIP-JOINT PLIERS

Slip-joint pliers are the most common and useful type of pliers.

The slip-joint plier has a pivot pin with two positions. In one position the jaw opening is wide to grip large parts. In the second position the jaw comes together leaving only enough space for small objects.

There are many sizes and varieties of the slip-joint plier. Most are between five and ten inches long and have jaw openings that range from one-half to one and one-half inches wide.

There are several types of pliers for many different uses

LOCKING PLIERS

Locking pliers are more commonly known as **vise** (vice) grips. The opening, or jaw, can be adjusted to different sizes. Once adjusted, the jaw will lock into position like a vise.

Because vise grips lock into position, they do not rely on hand power to hold tight. This makes it possible to use them to loosen a stuck nut.

Locking pliers can be used for many projects and are an important addition to any tool kit.

Vise grips are a useful type of pliers because they do not rely on hand power to hold tight

LONG NOSE PLIERS

Long nose pliers are sometimes called needle-nose pliers. This is because the tips of the jaw form a sharp point.

Long nose pliers are designed for **precision** (pree-SIZ-shun). Most are made for delicate work, like holding small objects or working with tiny wire.

Long nose pliers also have a section inside the jaw used to cut wire.

Needle-nose pliers are useful when working with crafting wire

It is important that an adult shows you the correct way to use any tool

Metal bars are melted down to make all kinds of tools

ELECTRICAL PLIERS

Pliers are an important tool for people who work with electrical wire. Lineman's sidecutters are the most common and useful type of electrical pliers.

An **electrician** (e-lek-TRISH-en) uses the end of the jaw on the pliers to bend and shape wire. If the wire needs to be cut, the electrician uses the cutting edge on the inside of the jaw.

The electrical pliers can easily cut soft metal, like copper and aluminum.

Bad weather forces electricians to rewire damaged traffic lights

PLIERS FOR MEDICAL USE

One type of pliers was designed for use by **surgeons** (SER-jenz), but is now used by many craftsmen. A **hemostat** (HE-mo-stat) is a precision tool made of stainless steel. The hemostat will clamp and hold onto most soft material.

Opticians (OP-tish-enz) use special pliers with padded jaws to hold and turn eyeglass lenses. The pads help to protect the lens from scratches.

Hemostats are special pliers used in an operating room

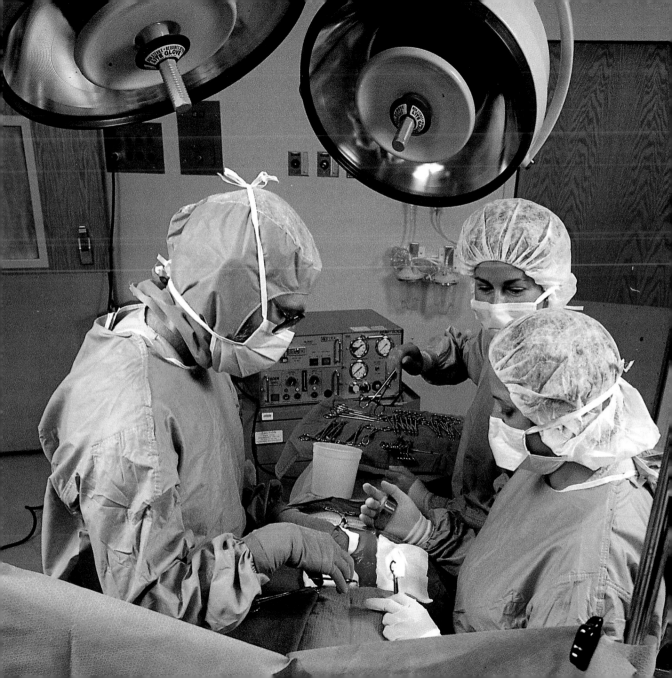

SPECIAL PLIERS

There are pliers designed for a specific purpose. Farmers use fence pliers to install and repair wire fences. Fence pliers can stretch and cut thick wire.

Some pliers are even made to enhance safety. Carpenters use offset pliers to grip a nail while striking it with a hammer. The offset pliers protect hands and fingers from injury.

Farmers use pliers whenever they need to repair broken wire fences

CARING FOR TOOLS

Tools that are well cared for will last a long time.

Pliers should be wiped clean with an oiled cloth to prevent rust. An occasional drop of oil on the pivot pin will keep the tool working smoothly.

If the edge of the jaw shows wear from use, it can be sharpened with a **file** (file). The steel ridges of the file are used to sharpen and to shape hard materials.

Astronauts use tools when working in space

SAFETY

Although pliers are not as dangerous as a saw or hammer, they can cause harm if not used properly.

Regular pliers should not be used in place of a wrench to loosen or tighten nuts. Pliers could slip and cause injury to fingers or hands.

It is important to wear safety glasses when working with pliers. Small parts can break away and fly into the air causing serious injury to unprotected eyes.

Glossary

electrician (e-lek-TRISH-en) — a person who designs, repairs, operates, or installs electrical equipment

file (file) — a steel tool used to sharpen, cut, or shape hard materials

hemostat (HE-mo-stat) — a tool usually used in the medical field for clamping soft materials

opticians (OP-tish-enz) — people who sell or make eye glasses and lenses

pivot (PIV-et) — a fixed pin on the end of which something turns

precision (pree-SIZ-shun) — the state of being accurate or exact

surgeons (SER-jenz) — doctors who specialize in repairing the injured

vise (vice) — a device that uses two jaws to hold or clamp

INDEX

cutting   5, 11, 14, 19
electrician   14
extension   5
file   20
handle   5
hemostat   16
injury   19, 22
jaw   5, 6, 9, 11, 14, 16, 20
nut   9, 22
opticians   16
pivot   5, 6, 20
pliers
   electrical pliers   14
   fence pliers   19

locking pliers   9
long nose pliers   11
offset pliers   19
slip joint pliers   6
precision   11, 16
safety   19
surgeons   16
vise   9
wire   11, 14, 19